D0016118

VOGUE KNITTING
FELTING

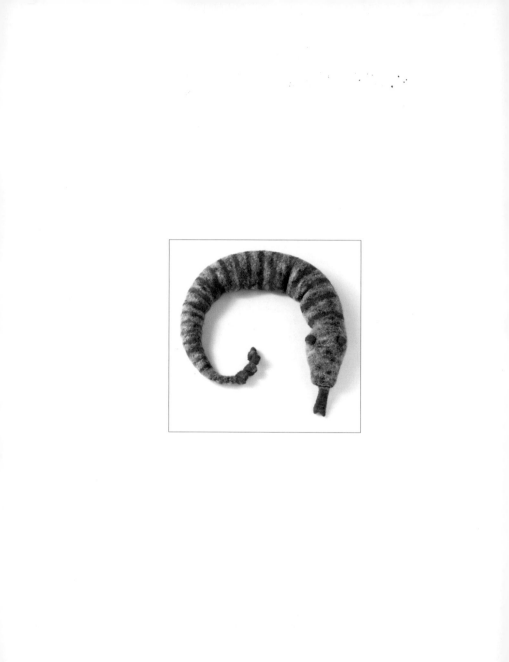

go!™

VOGUE KNITTING
FELTING

SIXTH&SPRING BOOKS
NEW YORK

SIXTH&SPRING BOOKS
233 Spring Street
New York, New York 10013

Library of Congress Cataloging-in-Publication Data

Felting.
     p. cm. -- (Vogue knitting on the go!)
     ISBN 1-931543-64-X
     1. Knitting--Patterns. 2.Felting. I. Series.

TT820.F455 2004
746.43'2--dc22   2004051772

Manufactured in China

1 3 5 7 9 10 8 6 4 2

First Edition, 2005

TABLE OF CONTENTS

INTRODUCTION

Have you ever washed your favorite wool sweater and it came out seven sizes too small? Have you ever wanted to hand knit a piece that is as durable as any machine knit item? If you answered YES to either of these questions it's time to start felting! Often times, pieces can be felted without you ever intending it, but for the projects in this book, you'll have fun as you purposely shrink down knitted items from bags to pillows.

There are many different techniques for felting, and these projects walk you through all the steps needed to create the simple yet fabulous desired result. Felting will make your wool hat extra warm, your knitted bag extra sturdy and your favorite slippers endure forever. Even the most inexperienced knitter can make a great looking felted piece, and the best part is, the felting process will cover any mistake!

Your felted pieces will last longer and you'll never have to worry about them slipping into the wash, because once felted—always felted. All the projects are made from 100% wool yarns, which is the only kind of feltable yarn, and will knit up in a flash to be ready to throw into the washer, or be felted by hand.

Get your next knitting project all set to take a bath—and get ready to **KNIT ON THE GO!**

THE BASICS

by Donna Druchunas

Felting is so easy, it can happen even when you don't want it to—as you already know if you've ever absentmindedly tossed a wool sweater in the washer and your beautiful cardigan comes out just the right size to fit your toddler. Heat, water, and agitation cause the scales of the fiber to open up. As the fibers move past each other during agitation, the scales catch and stick together. The fibers become locked and your soft, flexible hand-knitting turns into a dense, matted fabric. Felting is permanent; once the wool fibers mesh together, there is no way to separate them. Called "felt" or "boiled wool," the resulting fabric is amazingly durable.

When knitting felts accidentally, it is a disaster. But when you felt intentionally, you can create beautiful pieces with unusual textures that will stand up to the roughest handling, and that will not unravel even when cut in pieces. Felting also hides flaws in knitting, so even beginning knitters can have fun with this technique. Just sew up any misshapen or dropped stitches, and they will disappear in the washing machine.

Traditionally, the term "felting" refers to the technique of using wool fleece to create felt, while "fulling" refers to the technique of using knitted or woven pieces. Today, felting is commonly used for both techniques.

Felted projects allow you to be creative, but not all yarns can be used for felting. Only yarns made from natural animal fibers will felt. One-hundred percent wool, mohair, cashmere, llama and alpaca are all excellent choices. (If you're a hand-spinner, dog hair also felts nicely.) If you choose a blend, make sure it contains at least 80% wool or mohair.

Most bleached white wools do not felt, although some manufacturers do have white yarn that felts. Felt a test swatch to check. Pastel colors and heathers are sometimes also slow to felt because the wool is often bleached before it is dyed. Superwash, or machine-washable, wool yarn has been treated by the manufacturer to prevent felting. Acrylic, cotton, and plant fibers in general will not felt.

YARN SELECTION

Each item in this book has been knitted and felted with the yarn listed in the MATERIALS section of the pattern. For best results use the recommended yarn in the colors as shown. We've selected yarns

GAUGE

It is always important to knit a gauge swatch. In order to achieve the correct finished measurements after felting, it is imperative to get the gauge before felting and therefore we have only given the gauge before felting. If you knit to the suggested gauge, and felt according to the instructions, your project will turn out as intended.

Patterns usually state gauge over a 4"/10cm span; however, it's beneficial to make a larger test swatch. This gives a more precise stitch gauge, a better idea of the appearance and gives you a chance to familiarize yourself with the stitch pattern.

The type of needles used—straight or double pointed, wood or metal—will influence gauge, so knit your swatch with the needles you plan to use for the project.

Measure gauge as illustrated. Try different needle sizes until your sample measures the required number of stitches and rows. To get fewer stitches to the inch/cm, use larger needles; to get more stitches to the inch/cm, use smaller needles.

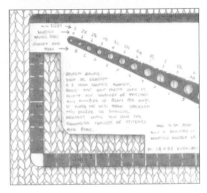

that are readily available in the U.S. and Canada at the time of printing. The Resources listed on page 86 provides addresses of the yarn distributors. Contact them for the name of a retailer in your area.

COLORWORK KNITTING

Two main types of colorwork are used in this book. If you choose to substitute the colors, or whenever you use multiple colors in a new felting project of your own design, be sure to knit and felt a swatch that uses all of the colors to make sure they don't run or shrink at different rates. See "Yarn Substitution" on page 14 for instructions on felting a swatch.

INTARSIA

Intarsia is accomplished with separate bobbins of individual colors. This method is ideal for large blocks of color or for motifs that aren't repeated close together. When changing colors, always pick up the new color and wrap around the old color to prevent holes.

Stranding

When motifs are closely placed, color work is accomplished by stranding along two or more colors per row. This technique normally creates "floats" on the wrong side of the fabric. Floats felt more quickly than plain knitting stitches and will distort the shape of the item. To eliminate the floats, weave the unused color between stitches.

Working with both hands, hold the main color in your right hand (English style) and the contrast color in your left hand (Continental style). To weave the yarn not in use, lift the index finger of your left hand so the yarn held there is above the working yarn and knit the next stitch. Move the yarn in your left hand below the working yarn and knit the next stitch.

FELTING

Each pattern in this book has specific felting instructions as written by the designers. For best results, we recommend that you follow those directions when felting your knitted project. The following is an overview of basic techniques.

Felting by Machine

Machine felting can be done in top loaders and in newer front loaders that allow you to open the door during the wash cycle. If you have an older front loader that locks during the wash cycle, you will not be able to check the felting progress to control the amount of shrinkage.

Place the knitted item in a zippered pillow case or mesh bag to catch any stray lint. Put the bag in the washing machine with an old pair of jeans or an old towel for added agitation. (Make sure the pockets are empty, any lint that gets into the felt will be stuck forever.) Set machine for smallest load size with a hot wash, and add a small amount of soap. Close the lid and turn on the machine.

Check the progress every five minutes until the desired size is achieved. Reset the agitation cycle if necessary. Some yarns may felt in a few minutes, while others may take several cycles.

When the fibers are matted and you don't want the item to shrink any more, take it out and gently rinse it in tepid water in the sink. Roll the item in a towel and squeeze out the excess water. Do NOT wring—it may pull the item out of shape!

SKILL LEVELS FOR KNITTING

■☐☐☐
Beginner
Ideal first project.

■■☐☐
Very Easy Very Vogue
Basic stitches, minimal shaping, simple finishing.

■■■☐
Intermediate
For knitters with some experience. More intricate stitches, shaping and finishing.

■■■■
Experienced
For knitters able to work patterns with complicated shaping and finishing.

Felting by Hand

Felting by hand is more labor intensive than felting by machine, but it wastes less water, particularly when you are felting a swatch or a small project.

Soak the finished item in hot water for thirty minutes or until it is completely saturated. Add a small amount of soap. Agitate the piece by rubbing and kneading. This may take some time, so be patient. If the water cools, add more hot water.

When the fibers are matted and you don't want the item to shrink any more, rinse it in tepid water. Roll item in a towel and squeeze out excess water. Do NOT wring—it may pull the item out of shape!

BLOCKING AND FINISHING

After felting and rinsing your item, trim off any stray ends that popped out during felting. If the edge of a piece flares and you can't flatten it by pressing, baste it with thread and gather the edge until it is flat. Remove the basting thread when the piece is dry.

- Block bags and hats using blocking forms, bowls, or plates.
- Shape mittens with your hand, and slippers with your foot.
- Small plastic bags work well for holding pieces in shape while drying. Once the felted item is shaped, gently stuff it with several crumpled bags.

- Steam press garment pieces and home décor items and block to pattern measurements. Using rustproof pins, pin the piece on a flat surface and allow to dry before removing the pins.

If the felted texture is too furry, use a dog or cat brush to make the fur on the surface of the felt stand up. Then cut the fur off using very sharp sewing shears to reveal the smooth, dense felt underneath. Be careful not to cut into the actual knitting.

CARE

Refer to the yarn label for the recommended cleaning method. Many of the projects in the book can be either washed by hand, or in the machine using no-rinse wool-wash soap. Do not agitate and don't soak for more than 10 minutes. (Agitating felted items in the washing machine may cause them to shrink more.) Fold in a towel and gently press the water out. Block and leave to air dry away from direct sunlight. To speed up the drying process, place the item near a heating vent or on top of the clothes dryer while it is use.

FIXING MISTAKES

Felting is an art, not a science. You may use the exact yarn specified in a project and follow the directions precisely, and still be surprised with the results of felting. Many times these "mistakes" can easily be fixed.

Too small. While the item is wet, stretch it.

Too big. Run the item through additional agitation cycles in the washing machine.

Too long. Cut bags or garment pieces to shorten. Embellish the cut edge with crochet or embroidery if desired.

Colors felt differently. Use hand felting to shrink the larger areas until they match the smaller areas.

Stranded colorwork areas shrink more than solid areas. While the item is wet, stretch the affected area.

Colors run. Carefully use Rit® Color Remover to clean the affected areas.

YARN SUBSTITUTION

Although it is best to use the recommended yarns in the colors as shown in this book, you may choose to substitute the yarns. Perhaps a spectacular yarn matches your favorite coat or an antique chair in your living room; maybe you view small-scale projects as a chance to incorporate leftovers from your yarn stash; or perhaps the yarn specified is not available in your area.

Some projects use a strand of wool held together with a strand of novelty yarn. The wool felts, locking the novelty yarn into place and creating beautiful and unique textures. You can substitute for both yarns as long as at least one of the strands is a fiber that will felt. Be sure to consider how different yarn types (wool, mohair, eyelash, etc.) will affect the final appearance of your project and how it will feel against your skin if used for a garment.

For an item to felt properly, your gauge should be loose enough so that you can see space between the stitches. If stitches are too tight, your piece may take a long time to felt and, even after a long period of agitation, may not shrink enough. Always knit and felt a gauge swatch before making a final decision about yarn substitution. After you've successfully knitted and felted the swatch with substitute yarn, you'll need to figure out how much of the substitute yarn the project requires. First, find the total length of the original yarn in the pattern (multiply the number of balls by yards/meters per ball). Divide this figure by the new yards/meters per ball (listed on the ball band). Round up to the next whole number. The answer is the number of balls required, but be sure to purchase extra yarn for swatching. Remember, once yarn has been felted, it cannot be reused.

To make a swatch for felting, cast on 30 sts and knit 40 rows in the pattern stitch used in your project. Both before and after you felt your swatch, measure its length and width.

Divide the width by 30 (number of stitches). This gives number of stitches per inch.

Divide the length by 40 (number of rows). This gives the number of rows per inch. You may not be able to see the stitches after the swatch is felted. This process allows you to measure the gauge after felting without being able to count stitches or rows.

Compare your felted test swatch to the finished measurements in the pattern to see if the yarn is suitable for the pattern.

If you plan to make a large item, always knit and felt a large test swatch. A small swatch will not give accurate results. However for a small item, work a small swatch. When substituting or trying a new pattern with expensive yarns, it is a good idea to test the shrinkage.

When substituting yarns—whether combining different yarns in one project or using different colors of the same yarn—felting a swatch is critical. The yarns or colors you have chosen may not felt at the same rate, or the colors may bleed onto each other.

FRINGE

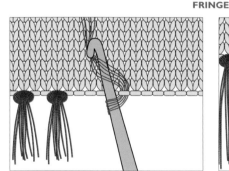

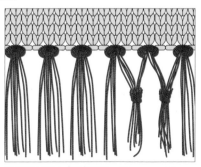

SIMPLE FRINGE: Cut yarn twice desired length plus extra for knotting. On wrong side, insert hook from front to back through piece and over folded yarn. Pull yarn through. Draw ends through and tighten. Trim yarn.

KNOTTED FRINGE: After working a simple fringe (it should be longer to allow for extra knotting), take one half of the strands from each fringe and knot them with half the strands from the neighboring fringe.

DOUBLE CAST ON

THREE-NEEDLE BIND-OFF

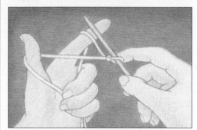

1 Make a slip knot on the right needle, leaving a long tail. Wind the tail end around your left thumb, front to back. Wrap the yarn from the ball over your left index finger and secure the ends in your palm.

1 With RS placed together, hold pieces on two parallel needles. Insert a third needle knitwise into the first stitch of each needle, and wrap the yarn around the needle as if to knit.

2 Insert the needle upwards in the loop on your thumb. Then with the needle, draw the yarn from the ball through the loop to form a stitch.

2 Knit these two stitches together, and slip them off the needles. *Knit the next two stitches together in the same manner.

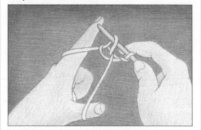

3 Take your thumb out of the loop and tighten the loop on the needle. Continue in this way until all the stitches are cast on.

3 Slip the first stitch on the third needle over the second stitch and off the needle. Repeat from the * in Step 2 across the row until all stitches have been bound off.

KNIT SIDE

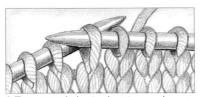

1 To prevent holes in the piece and create a smooth transition, wrap a knit stitch as follows: With the yarn in back, slip the next stitch purlwise.

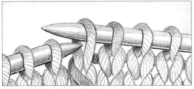

2 Move the yarn between the needles to the front of the work.

3 Slip the same stitch back to the left needle. Turn the work, bringing the yarn to the purl side between the needles. One stitch is wrapped.

4 When you have completed all the short rows, you must hide the wraps. Work to just before the wrapped stitch. Insert the right needles under the wrap and knitwise into the wrapped stitch. Knit them together.

PURL SIDE

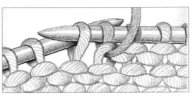

1 To prevent holes in the piece and to create a smooth transition, wrap a purl stitch as follows: With the yarn in front, slip the next stitch purlwise.

2 Slip the same stitch back to the left needle. Turn the work, bringing the yarn back to the purl side between the needles. One stitch is wrapped.

3 Move the yarn between the needles to the back of the work.

4 After working the short rows, you must hide the wraps. Work to just before the wrapped stitch. Insert the right needle from behind into the back loop of the wrap and place it on the left needle, as shown. Purl it together with the stitch on the left needle.

KNITTING TERMS AND ABBREVIATIONS

approx approximately

beg begin(ning)

bind off Used to finish an edge and keep stitches from unraveling. Lift the first stitch over the second, the second over the third, etc. (UK: cast off)

cast on A foundation row of stitches placed on the needle in order to begin knitting.

CC contrast color

ch chain(s)

cm centimeter(s)

cn cable needle

cont continu(e)(ing)

dc double crochet (UK: tr-treble)

dec decrease(ing)—Reduce the stitches in a row (knit 2 together).

dpn double pointed needle(s)

foll follow(s)(ing)

g gram(s)

garter stitch Knit every row. Circular knitting: knit one round, then purl one round.

hdc half-double crochet (UK: htr-half treble)

inc increase(ing)—Add stitches in a row (knit into the front and back of a stitch).

k knit

k2tog knit 2 stitches together

lp(s) loops(s)

LH left-hand

m meter(s)

M1 make one stitch—With the needle tip, lift the strand between last stitch worked and next stitch on the left-hand needle and knit into the back of it. One stitch has been added.

MC main color

mm millimeter(s)

oz ounce(s)

p purl

p2tog purl 2 stitches together

pat pattern

pick up and knit (purl) Knit (or purl) into the loops along an edge.

pm place marker—Place or attach a loop of contrast yarn or purchased stitch marker as indicated.

rem remain(s)(ing)

rep repeat

rev St st reverse Stockinette stitch— Purl right-side rows, knit wrong-side rows. Circular knitting: purl all rounds. (UK: reverse stocking stitch)

rnd(s) round(s)

RH right-hand

RS right side(s)

sc single crochet (UK: dc - double crochet)

sk skip

SKP Slip 1, knit 1, pass slip stitch over knit 1.

SK2P Slip 1, knit 2 together, pass slip stitch over k2tog.

sl slip—An unworked stitch made by passing a stitch from the left-hand to the right-hand needle as if to purl.

sl st slip stitch (UK: single crochet)

ssk slip, slip, knit—Slip next 2 stitches knitwise, one at a time, to right-hand needle. Insert tip of left-hand needle into fronts of these stitches from left to right. Knit them

together. One stitch has been decreased.

st(s) stitch(es)

St st Stockinette stitch—Knit right-side rows, purl wrong-side rows. Circular knitting: knit all rounds. (UK: stocking stitch)

tbl through back of loop

tog together

tr treble crochet (UK: dtr-double treble)

WS wrong side(s)

w&t wrap and turn

wyif with yarn in front

wyib with yarn in back

work even Continue in pattern without increasing or decreasing. (UK: work straight)

yd yard(s)

yo yarn over—Make a new stitch by wrapping the yarn over the right-hand needle. (UK: yfwd, yon, yrn)

* Repeat directions following * as many times as indicated.

[ ] Repeat directions inside brackets as many times as indicated.

■■■◻

Keep the winter chills at bay with a little rattler by **Victoria Hilditch**. His silly stripes and sassy tongue will make him a family favorite.

KNITTED MEASUREMENTS

■ Before felting: 54"/138cm
■ After felting: approx 36"/91.5cm from mouth to beginning of I-cord tail

MATERIALS

■ 2 3½oz/100g hanks (each approx 152yd/138m) of Colinette Yarns/Unique Kolours *Skye* (wool) in #102 Pierro (MC)
■ 1 hank in #71 Fire (A)
■ Scrap yarn
■ One pair size 10½ (6.5mm) straight needles *or size to obtain gauge*
■ One set size 10½ (6.5mm) double pointed needles for I-cord
■ Stitch markers
■ Tapestry needle
■ Approx 4 bags dried lentils or other small dried beans
■ Funnel

GAUGE

16 sts and 18 rows = 4"/10cm over St st using size 10½ (6.5mm) needles (before felting).
Knit and felt gauge swatch as per felting directions below.

Notes
1 Body of snake is worked in striped pat-tern; tail, eyes and tongue are worked in A.
2 Snake is worked from base of tail, ending with mouth and tongue. Tail is worked in I-cord after body is completed.

STRIPE PATTERN
All stripe pats are worked in St st.
Stripe Pat 1
Row 1 (RS) With A, knit.
Row 2 With A, purl.
Row 3 and 5 With MC, knit.
Row 4 and 6 With MC, purl.
Rep rows 1-6 a total of 10 times—60 rows, then begin stripe pat 2.
Stripe Pat 2
Row 1 and 3 (RS) With A, knit.
Row 2 With A, purl.
Rows 4 , 6 and 8 With MC, purl.
Rows 5, 7 and 9 With MC, knit.
Rows 10 and 12 With A, purl.
Row 11 With A, knit.
Rows 13, 15 and 17 With MC, knit.
Rows 14, 16 and 18 With MC, purl.
Rep rows 1-18 a total of 4 times—72 rows, then begin stripe pat 3.
Stripe Pat 3
Rows 1 and 3 (RS) With A, knit.
Rows 2 and 4 With A, purl.
Rows 5, 7, 9, 11 With MC, knit.
Rows 6, 8, 10, 12 With MC, purl.
Rep rows 1-12 a total of 6 times—72 rows, then work in MC only.

STITCH GLOSSARY
Inc Row 1 (RS) K to marker, slip marker, M1, k to marker, M1, slip marker, k to

marker, slip maker, M1, k to marker, M1, slip maker, k to end (4 sts inc'd.)

Inc Row 2 (RS) K to marker, M1, slip marker, k to marker, slip maker, M1, k to marker, M1, slip maker, k to marker, slip marker, M1, k to end (4 sts inc'd.)

Dec Row 1 (RS) K to 2 sts before marker, k2tog, slip mark, k to marker, slip marker, ssk, k to 2 sts before marker, k2tog, slip marker, k to marker, slip marker, ssk, k to end (4 sts dec'd.)

Dec Row 2 (RS) *K to 2 sts before marker, k2tog, slip marker, ssk; rep from * 3 times more, k to end (8 sts dec'd.)

MAKE BOBBLE (MB)
With A, make 5 sts in next st. (Turn and knit these 5 sts) five times to make 5 rows in bobble. **Next row** K5 tog—1 bobble made.

SNAKE DRAFT DODGER
With straight needles and scrap yarn, cast on 11 sts. Change to A.

Next row (WS) P2, pm, p3, pm, p1, pm, p3, pm, p2. Beg stripe pat 1 and work even for 10 rows.

Note

Purl all WS rows, and sl all markers.

Next row (RS) Cont in stripe pat 1 and work inc row 1—15 sts. Cont to work in stripe pat 1 and rep inc row 1 every 10th row twice more—23 sts. Work even for 11 rows.

Next row (RS) Work inc row 2—27 sts. Rep inc row 2 every 12th row 5 times more—47 sts. Work even on 47 sts until 192 rows from beg, then shape neck and head, AT SAME TIME, when 60 rows of stripe pat 1 are completed, beg stripe pat 2, then when 72 rows of stripe pat 2 are completed, begin to work stripe pat 3. When 72 rows of stripe pat 3 are completed, work in MC only.

Shape neck and head

Next row (RS) Work dec row 1—43 sts. Work 5 rows even.

Next row (RS) Work dec row 1—39 sts. Work 5 rows even.

Next row (RS) Work inc row 1—43 sts. Work 3 rows even.

Next row (RS) Work inc row 2—47 sts. Work 3 rows even.

Eyes

Next row (RS) With MC: k to 1 st before second marker, with A: MB, slip marker, with MC: k to next marker, slip marker, with A: MB, with MC: k to end. Work 3 rows even.

Shape mouth

Next row (RS) With MC, work dec row 2—39 sts. Rep dec row 2 every 10th row twice more—23 sts. Remove markers. Work 3 rows even.

Next row (RS) K4, [k2tog] 3 times, k3, [ssk] 3 times, k4—17 sts. Work 1 row even.

Next row (RS) K4, bind off 9 sts, k to

end—8 sts. Place rem 8 sts on holders, sew center seam, matching stripes. Place 8 sts tog on 1 needle as if for RS row, with center seam facing.

Tongue

Next row (RS) With A, ssk, k1, k2 center sts tog, k1, k2 tog—5 sts. Work 16 rows garter st. Bind off.

Tail

Unravel scrap yarn from cast on row and place 11 sts on 1 double pointed needle as for a RS row. Cont with two dpn as foll:

Next row (RS) With A, k2tog, k to last 2 sts, k2tog—9 sts. Work I-cord for 15"/38cm.

Next rnd *K1, k2tog, rep from * twice more—6 sts.

Next rnd *K1, k2 tog, k1, k2tog—4 sts.

Next rnd K1, k2 tog, k1—3 sts.

Next rnd K3tog — 1 st. Pull yarn through rem st. Trim.

Set washer for small load, regular cycle, hot water and cold rinse. Place snake in large mesh bag. Place an old towel (for agitation) and snake in machine with soap flakes. Run load. When machine finishes, remove snake from bag. If sts are not visible, proceed to shape for drying as below. If necessary, run machine again on short cycle, but check felting progress frequently. Remove snake as soon as knit sts are no longer visible. Stuff plastic bags into snake through mouth opening, but do not stretch the snake fabric. Shape middle of body to be circular, and tail end of body to be box-like. Head should be shaped so that eyes are positioned on top of head. When dry carefully remove bags. Using funnel, slowly fill snake with beans through mouth opening. Sew mouth closed, leaving tongue out. Make cut in center of tongue tip to make forked tongue.

Tiny tote

■■■▪▢

Keep your essentials near and dear with this sweet and simple Janet Scanlon design, made with hand-dyed mohair, silk and bouclé yarn.

KNITTED MEASUREMENTS
■ Before felting: 3¾"/9.5cm x 1¼"/3cm x 7¼"/18.5cm
■ After felting: approx 3½"/9cm x ¾"/2cm x 3¾"/9.5cm

MATERIALS
■ 1 2oz /70g skein (each approx 650yd/585m) of LaLana Wools *Como Bouclé* (wool) in Mullein (MC)
■ 1 2oz /70g skein (each approx 142yd/31m) of *Phat Silk Fine* (wool) in Madder (A)
■ 1 2oz /70g skein (each approx 118yd/108m) Forever Random Fines *Glacé* (wool) in Dreamtime (B)
■ 1 2oz/70g skein (each approx 950yd/855m) of Forever Random Fines *Mohair Accent* in Sherwood Forest (C)
■ One pair size 11 (8 mm) needles *or size to obtain gauge*
■ One set (3) size 11 (8 mm) double pointed needles
■ Size 10 (6mm) circular needle, 24"/60cm long
■ Tapestry needle
■ One ¾"/2 cm button
■ Stitch marker

GAUGE
11 sts and 16 rows = 4"/10cm over St st in MC, using larger needles (before felting). *Take time to check gauge.*

Note
Bag is worked back and forth in rows for flap, then worked in rounds. Strap is worked back and forth in rows.

STITCH GLOSSARY
SSKP Slip 2 sts one at a time knitwise, knit the next st, pass the 2 sl sts over the knit st—2 sts decreased.

FLAP
With larger needles and MC, cast on 10 sts.
K 2 rows.
*With 1 strand A and B held tog, k 2 rows.
With MC, k 4 rows. Rep from * twice more. With MC, k 2 rows.

BAG
Using MC and cable cast on, cast on 18 additional sts—28 sts.
Divide sts evenly onto 2 dpns—14 sts each.
Taking care not to twist sts, arrange needles so that they are parallel to each other, with the yarn hanging from the RH end of back needle. Pm on cast on row to mark beg of rnd. With third dpn, knit the first st of the front needle, pulling yarn snug to close the circle.
Rnds 1-8 With MC, knit.
Rnd 9 With B and C held tog, knit.
Rnd 10 With B and C held tog, purl.
Rnd 11 With 2 strands of A held tog, knit.

Rnd 12 With B and C held tog, knit.
Rnd 13 With B and C held tog, purl.
Cut accent colors. With MC, k for 12 rnds — approx 3"/8cm.
Shape bag
Next rnd Sskp, k8, sskp, sskp, k8, sskp— 10 st rem on each needle.
Next rnd Knit. Bind off using 3 needle bind off.

STRAP
With circular needle and C, cast on 180 sts, using cable cast on.
Row 1 Knit.
Rows 2 and 3 With B, knit.
Row 4 With C, bind off.

FELTING
Put items in separate zippered pillowcases/ mesh bags. Set washer for low water level and hottest temperature. Add small amount of soap and items to be felted. Put through wash cycle, checking felting progress often. When desired size, remove from machine and rinse in cool water to remove soap and to stop felting process. Roll in dry towel to remove excess water. Shape as desired and gently stuff with a plastic bag to dry.

FINISHING
When dry, use tip of dpn to make a hole on each side of bag, just above accent stripe. Insert strap end into hole, knot strap on inside of bag to desired length. Twist 2 strands of C tog, make new strand 2"/5cm long. Knot strand, make loop and sew to bottom edge of front flap for button loop. Sew button to center front of bag, in middle of accent strip.

Mauve madness

■■■▭

This Van Gogh-inspired fare isn't your typical cushion. A distinctive work that is sure to become a conversation piece, it uses felted pieces instead of knitted fabric. Designed by Sasha Kagan.

KNITTED MEASUREMENTS
15" x 11"/ 38cm x 28cm

MATERIALS
- Kitchen towel 19" x 15"/48.5cm x 38cm
- Piece of muslin 19" x 15"/48.5cm x 38cm
- Piece of netting 19" x 15"/48.5cm x 38cm
- Piece of purple fabric for cushion back 16" x 12"/41cm x 30.5cm
- 1 pillow form 15" x 11"/38cm x 28cm Merino wool combed tops; 1 hank each in pale lilac, mauve, peach, purple and navy blue
- Wensleydale uncombed crinkled fleece in bright pink
- Rowan/Westminster summer tweed in #528 Brilliant and #525 blueberry
- Small tub to fit 15" x 11"/38cm x 28cm
- Plastic bowl
- Soap flakes

FRONT
Cut Merino Wool tops into 6"/15cm lengths and separate fibers.
Layer I
Place kitchen towel in tub, spread out flat. Spread muslin on top of kitchen towel.

Place approx 1/3 of pale lilac and mauve fibers across muslin, from top to bottom, blending colors.
Layer 2
Place approx 1/3 of pale lilac and mauve fibers across Layer 1, from side to side, blending colors.
Layer 3
Work in same manner as for Layer 1, blending colors in following sequence: navy blue, purple, mauve, pale lilac, peach. Separate the pink Wensleydale crinkle fleece and lay the fibers across Layer 3, in fragmented horizontal stripes (use photo as guide).

FELTING
Place netting on top of Layer 3. Pour small amount of hot water over netting. Gently work in soap flakes, using circular motion from center to outside edges. Open up fibers gently, using more water and soap, if needed. Try not to disturb design. Rub harder with palm of hand for 10-15 minutes.

SHRINKING
Fold the piece in half carefully, letting excess water drain out into tub. Do not squeeze or wring. Take folded piece and throw repeatedly and forcibly into plastic bowl for 10 minutes. Open piece carefully and separate muslin from kitchen towel. Carefully peel away net from top of layers and ease into rectangular shape (16" x 12"/41.5cm x 31cm). Lay flat to dry.

FINISHING

With right sides facing, place purple cushion back fabric with felted wool piece. Pin together and trim wool edges, if necessary. Sew fabrics together on 3 sides, with 1"/2.5cm seam allowance. Turn right side out, insert pillow form. Sew rem side closed.

CORDS (make 2 each color)

Twist together 2 strands of brilliant to make 17"/43.5cm cord, make knots 1"/2.5cm from both ends. Sew to top and bottom edges of cushion, leaving knots to hang off corner. With 2 strands blueberry, make 14"/36cm cords and sew to sides of cushion in same manner as above.

EMBROIDERED BAG
Pocket posey

■■□▷

With tweedy dimension and retro embroidered flowers, this compact hand bag is pretty in pink. Designed by Linda Medina.

KNITTED MEASUREMENTS
- Before felting: 9½"/24cm x 11½"/29cm
- After felting: 8½"/21.5cm x 9"/23cm

MATERIALS
- 2 3½oz/100g skeins (each approx 183yd/167m) of Tahki Yarns/Tahki•Stacy Charles, Inc., *Donegal Tweed* (wool) in #818 pink
- One pair size 8 (5mm) needles *or size to obtain gauge*
- Two size 8 (5mm) dpn for I-cord
- A few yards each of tapestry wool in blue, burgundy, dark sage green, and antique gold
- Tapestry needle
- Tissue paper/tear away stabilizer for embroidery

GAUGE
17 sts and 24 rows = 4"/10cm over St st using size 8 needles (before felting).
Take time to check gauge.

Make swatch
Cast on 27 sts, knit 6 rows. Change to St st and work for 24 rows. Knit 6 rows, bind off. Place swatch in pillowcase and close securely. Wash in machine with a few tow-els and hot water, repeat. Dry with towels in hot dryer, remove while still damp, pat into shape. Allow to dry. Swatch should measure 6"/15.5cm by 4"/10cm.

BACK
Cast on 40 sts. Knit 8 rows. Work 58 rows St st. Knit 8 rows. Bind off.

FRONT
Work as for back.

STRAPS
(make 2)
With dpn, cast on 4 sts and work I-cord as foll: ***Next row (RS)** K4, do not turn work. Slide sts to beg of needle to work next row from RS. Rep from * until cord measures 74"/188cm. Bind off.

FELTING
Place each piece in separate case and felt as for swatch.

FINISHING
Copy embroidery design onto paper and baste on Front. Work embroidery, follow-ing diagram. Sew I-cords tog, lengthwise. Knot one end. Place knot at lower corner of front, sew strap to side edge of front. Make knot at top corner of front. Sew back to strap in same way. Sew strap to other side of front and then back, do not twist strap. Sew bottom edges of front and back tog.

Small Flower – Burgundy satin stitch petals with 3 antique gold French knots in center
Large Flower – Blue satin petals with 3 or 4 antique gold French knots in center
Leaves – Dark sage green fly stitch
Stems & "point" end of leaves – Dark sage green stem stitch
Scattered French knots – antique gold, blue and burgundy

■■■■

With this delightful project featuring authentic lace and embroidery details, Therese Chynoweth pays homage to a classic victorian quilting technique.

KNITTED MEASUREMENTS

■ Before felting: 21"/53cm x 31.5"/80cm
■ After felting: approx 16"/40.5cm x 12"/30.5cm

MATERIALS

■ 2 1¾oz/50g balls (each approx 109yds/100m) of Dale of Norway *Heilo* (wool) in #5764 indigo (MC)
■ 1 ball each in #2671 dark taupe (A), #4845 dark plum (B), #5744 norwegian blue (C) and #8972 dark olive (D)
■ One pair size 8 (5mm) needles or *size to obtain gauge*
■ 2 hanks (each approx 8½yd/8m) of DMC floss (cotton) in #223 light shell pink, #414 dark steel grey and #3347 medium yellow green
■ 1 hank in #312 very dark baby blue, #816 garnet and #3032 medium mocha brown
■ 1 spool (each approx 55yd/50m) of Kreinik *Silk Serica* (silk) in #2017 very dark gold and #4077 very dark dusty green
■ 1 card (each approx 3yd/2.7m) of Bucilla *100% Pure Silk ribbon* (silk) in #009 lilac and #540 dusty rose
■ 1yd/1m of lace approx 1¾"/4.5cm wide
■ Size 6/0 seed beads in mixed colors
■ One 14"/35.5cm zipper
■ One pillow form to fit 16"/40.5cm x 12"/30.5cm

■ Embroidery needle
■ Bobbins

GAUGE

17 sts and 23 rows = 4"/10cm over chart pattern (before felting).
Take time to check gauge.

Note

When changing colors, twist yarns on WS to prevent holes in work. Use a separate bobbin of yarn for each large block of color.

PILLOW

With C, cast on 90 sts.
Work in St st and chart pat until rows 1-90 have been worked twice. Bind off with C.

FINISHING

Work in ends. Fold pillow in half at beg of second rep with right sides facing tog. Sew side seams. Sew approx 2"/5cm seam along each side of lower edge, leaving center open for zipper.

FELTING

Put pillow in zippered pillowcase or mesh bag. Set washer for low water level and hottest temperature. Add small amount of soap and pillow. Put through wash cycle, checking felting progress often. When desired size, remove from machine and rinse in cool water to remove soap and to stop felting process. Roll in dry towel to remove excess water. Shape as desired and gently stuff with a plastic bag to dry.

Following embroidery chart and using photo as guide, embroider on both sides of pillow. Cut lace into 6 pieces, each approx 6"/15.5cm long. Gather and fold lower edge into pleats, forming lace into fan shapes and fold ends of lace to WS. Pin and sew 3 lace fans to each side of pillow as shown in photo. Work 16 french knots (8 of each color) at lower edge of each fan. Sew zipper into opening.

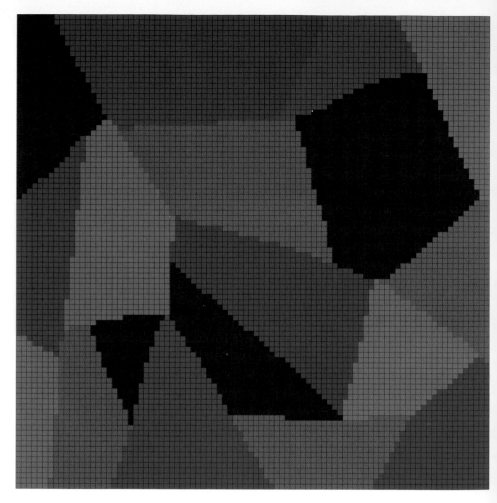

Color Key

 Indigo (MC)

Dark taupe (A)

Dark plum (B)

Norwegian blue (C)

Dark olive(D)

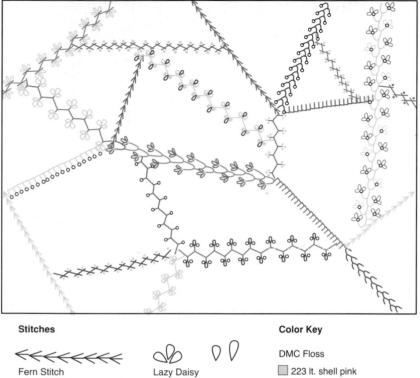

Stitches

Fern Stitch

Herringbone Stitch

Chevron Stitch

Cretan Stitch

Buttonhole/Blanket Stitch

Featherstitch

Lazy Daisy

French Knots

○ Bead

Color Key

DMC Floss

☐ 223 lt. shell pink

■ 312 very dk baby blue

■ 414 dk steel grey

■ 816 garnet

■ 3032 med. mocha brown

☐ 3347 medium yellow green

Kreinik Silk Serica

☐ 2017 Very dark gold

■ 4077 Very dark dusty green

BERET
French connection

■■■■▭

The beauty of classic French styling is perfected with this felted beret knit in a spiral ridge pattern. Designed by Mari Lynn Patrick.

KNITTED MEASUREMENTS
- Diameter before felting: 12"/30.5cm
- Diameter after felting: 10½"/27cm

MATERIALS
- 1 1¾oz/50g ball (each approx 130yd/120m) of Berroco *Pleasure* (angora/wool/nylon) in #8617 lt green (A)
- 1 1½oz/43g ball (each approx 93yd/85m) of Berroco *Classic Mohair Heather* (wool/mohair/nylon) in #A9544 lt green heather (B)
- One set (5) dpn, size 11 (8mm) *or size to obtain gauge*
- Size 10 (6mm) circular needle, 24"/60cm long
- Size I/9 (5.5mm) crochet hook
- Stitch marker
- One 12"/30.5cm round dinner plate

GAUGE
12 sts and 16 rnds to 4"/10cm over pat st using size 11 (8mm) needle and 1 strand A and B held tog (before felting).
Take time to check gauge.

Pattern Stitch (multiple of 4 sts)
Rnd 1 *K2, p2; rep from * around.
Rnds 2 and 4 K the knit sts and p the purl sts.
Rnd 3 *P2, k2; rep from * around.
Rep rnds 1-4 for pat st.

Note
Beret is worked in the round with 1 strand of A and B held tog throughout.

BERET
Beg at top center, with 1 strand A and B held tog, and size I/9 (5.5mm) crochet hook, ch 4, join with sl st to form ring.
Rnd 1 Using crochet hook to pull loops through ch ring, pull up 8 loops in ring and place evenly divided onto 4 dpn, taking care not to twist sts. Pm to mark beg of rnd.
Rnd 2 K1 into front and back of each st around—16 sts.
Rnd 3 [K1, inc 1 st in next st] 8 times—24 sts.
Rnd 4 Purl.
Rnd 5 [K2, inc 1 st in next st] 8 times—32 sts.
Rnd 6 [K3, inc 1 st in next st] 8 times—40 sts.
Rnd 7 [K4, inc 1 st in next st] 8 times—48 sts.
Rnd 8 Purl.
Rnd 9 [K5, inc 1 st in next st] 8 times—56 sts.
Rnd 10 [K6, inc 1 st in next st] 8 times—64 sts.
Rnd 11 [K7, inc 1 st in next st] 8 times—72 sts.
Rnd 12 Purl.
Rnd 13 [K11, inc 1 st in next st] 6 times—78 sts.
Rnd 14 [K12, inc 1 st in next st] 6 times—84 sts.

Rnd 15 Knit.

Rnds 16 and 17 [K2, p2] 21 times.

Rnds 18 and 19 [P2, k2] 21 times.

Rep rnds 16-19 a total of 3 more times.

Then rep rnds 16 and 17 once.

Change to size 10 (6mm) circular needle.

Next rnd *K2, p2, k2tog, k1, p2, k2, p2tog, p1; rep from * around—72 sts.

Work even in k2, p2 rib for 7 more rnds.

Last rnd *K2, p2tog; rep from * around—54 sts. Bind off.

FELTING

Step 1 Immerse beret in water, then roll in a towel to remove excess water. Using a 12"/30.5cm dinner plate, let beret dry while stretched over plate.

Step 2 Using low level, hot water setting and delicate cycle, place beret in standard washing machine with ½ measure of detergent. Put through wash cycle. Place beret in clothes dryer on normal setting and put through dry cycle.

BUCKET BAG
City sack

■■■◻

An urban design that makes it uptown or downtown, this quick knit in the round is rich in variegated color and features modern styling appropriate for day or night. From Anne Whitenight Handknitting Originals.

KNITTED MEASUREMENTS
■ Before felting: 36½"/93cm circumference, 17"/43cm tall
■ After felting approx 26"/66cm circumference, 9"/23cm tall

MATERIALS
■ 3 3½oz/100g hanks (each approx 110yd/100m) Muench Yarns *Black Forest Tweed* (wool) in #T2-02 black
■ Size 11 (8mm) circular needle 24"/60cm long *or size to obtain gauge*
■ 3 long stitch holders
■ Tapestry needle

GAUGE
11 sts and 16 rows = 4"/10cm on size 11 (8mm) needles (before felting).
Take time to check gauge.

Note
Handbag body is knit in the round on circular needle. When body of bag is complete, the bottom segments are worked back and forth in rows, then seamed before felting.

HANDBAG
Cast on 100 sts. Pm to mark beg rnds.

Being careful not to twist sts, join work to knit in rnds.
Rnds 1-15 Knit.
Shape handle
Rnd 16 K15, bind off 20 sts, k until there are 30 sts from bind-off, bind off 20 sts, k15.
Rnd 17 K15, cast on 20 sts, k30, cast on 20 sts, k15.
Rnds 18 to 67 Knit.
Rnd 68 Knit 25 sts for one section of bottom, sl the next 25 sts onto one holder, sl the next 25 sts onto second holder, and last 25 sts onto third holder, all to be worked later.
Shape bottom
(work back and forth in rows)
Next row (WS) P25.
Row 1 K2, ssk, k to last 4 sts, SKP, k2—23 sts.
Row 2 and all WS rows Purl.
Rep rows 1 and 2 eight times—7 sts
Row 19 K1, ssk, k1, SKP, k1—5 sts.
Row 21 Ssk, k1, SKP—3 sts.
Place rem 3 sts on holder. Cut yarn.
*Slip 25 sts from holder onto needle ready for RS row. Join yarn and k 1 row, p 1 row. Work rows 1-21 as for first bottom section. Rep from * for the rem two 25 st sections, cut 11"/30cm yarn on last section. Pull yarn through remaining 12 sts, tie off.

FINISHING
Loosely whip stitch the 4 bottom sections tog to close bottom. Weave in loose ends.

FELTING

Put bag in zippered pillowcase or mesh bag. Set washer for low water level and hottest temperature. Add small amount of soap and bag. Put through wash cycle, checking felting progress often. When desired size, remove from machine and rinse in cool water to remove soap and to stop felting process. Roll in dry towel to remove excess water. Shape as desired and gently stuff with a plastic bag to dry.

■■■■▶

Sturdy by nature and pretty by design, these Vicki Sever mittens use modular fans to mimic striking stained glass cathedral windows.

SIZE
To fit adult woman's sizes.

KNITTED MEASUREMENTS
- Before felting: 4¾"/12cm x 11"/28cm
- After felting 4"/10cm x 9"/23.5cm

MATERIALS
- 1 3½oz/100g hank (each approx 138yd/126m) of Manos del Uruguay (wool) each in Turquoise (A) and #58 Gold (B) or #61 Rhubarb (A) and #109 Woodland (B)
- One pair size 10½ (6.5mm) needles *or size to obtain gauge*
- One set (4) size 10½ (6.5mm) dpn
- Five small stitch holders or safety pins

GAUGE
15 sts and 20 rows to 4"/10cm over St st using size 10½ (6.5mm) needles (before felting). *Take time to check gauge.*

Notes
Mittens are worked in modular fan pieces, each fan is picked up along the edges of the adjoining fans. Follow diagram for fan placement. Mittens are worked from top to bottom. Note that some fans call to pick up sts, others call for pick up and knit stitches. Pick up sts means to pick up lps from edge to work as sts; pick up and knit means to pull yarn through edge sts to make sts.

STITCH GLOSSARY
Pattern 1 (beg with 18 sts)
Row 1 (WS) With A, k18.
Rows 2 and 4 With B, k1tbl, k16, wyif sl 1.
Rows 3 and 5 With B, k1tbl, p16, wyif sl 1.
Row 6 With A, k1tbl, [k2tog] 8 times, wyif sl 1—10 sts.
Row 7 With A, k1tbl, k8, wyif sl 1.
Row 8 With B, k1tbl, k2tog, k4, ssk, wyif sl 1— 8 sts.
Row 9 With B, k1tbl, p6, wyif sl 1.
Row 10 With B, k1tbl, k2tog, k2, ssk, wyif sl 1— 6 sts.
Row 11 With B, k1tbl, p4, wyif sl 1.
Row 12 With A, k1tbl, k2tog, ssk, wyif sl 1—4 sts.
Row 13 With A, k1tbl, k2, wyif sl 1.
Row 14 With A, ssk, k2tog—2 sts.
Pattern 2 (beg with 16 sts)
Row 1 (WS) With A, k15, wyif sl 1.
Rows 2 and 4 With B, k1tbl, k14, wyif sl 1.
Rows 3 and 5 With B, k1tbl, p14, wyif sl 1.
Row 6 With A, k1tbl, [k2tog, k2tog, k1] twice, [k2tog] twice, wyif sl 1—10 sts.
Row 7 With A, k1tbl, k8, wyif, sl 1.
Row 8 With B, k1tbl, k2tog, k4, ssk, wyif sl 1—8 sts.
Row 9 With B, k1tbl, p6, wyif sl 1.
Row 10 With B, k1tbl, k2tog, k2, ssk, wyif sl 1—6 sts.
Row 11 With B, k1tbl, p4, wyif sl 1.
Row 12 With A, k1tbl, k2tog, ssk, wyif sl 1—4 sts.

Row 13 With A, k1tbl, k2, wyif sl 1—sts.
Row 14 With A, ssk, k2tog—2 sts.
Pattern 3 (beg with 16 sts)
Row 1 (WS) With A, k15, wyif sl 1.
Row 2 With B, k1tbl, k2tog, k10, ssk, wyif sl 1—14 sts.
Row 3 With B, k1tbl, p12, wyif sl 1.
Row 4 With B, k1tbl, k2tog, k8, ssk, wyif sl 1—12 sts.
Row 5 With B, k1tbl, p10, wyif sl 1.
Row 6 With A, k1tbl, [k2tog] 5 times, wyif sl 1— 7 sts.
Row 7 With A, k1tbl, k6.

MITTENS
(make 2, working each the same through Fan 9)

MITTEN TOP
Fan 1 Using backward loop method and A, cast on 18 sts. Work Pat 1, place rem 2 sts on holder.
Fan 2 With RS facing and A, pick up 18 lps along cast—on edge of Fan 1. Work Pat 1, place rem 2 sts on holder.
Fan 3 With RS of Fan 1 facing and A, beg at st holder and pick up 16 lps along common top edge of Fans 1 and 2, end at next st holder. Work Pat 2, place rem 2 sts on holder.
Fan 4 Rep as for Fan 3 along other common top edge of Fans 1 and 2, place rem 2 sts on holder.
Fan 5 With RS of Fan 3 facing and A, beg at Fan 3 st holder and pick up and k 7 sts along top edge of Fan 3, k 2 sts from Fan 1 st holder, pick up and k 7 sts along top edge of Fan 4 to next st holder—16 sts. Work Pat 2, place 2 rem st on holder.
Fans 6-9 Rep as for Fan 5, use Fan Diagram as guide.
Fan 10 Make thumb hole as foll:

RIGHT HAND
With A, pick up and k 7 sts along edge of Fan 8, k 2 sts from Fan 6 st holder. Using backward loop method, cast on 6 sts (skip over first 6 sts of edge of Fan 7), pick up and k 1 st in the 7th edge st (the one next to the holder on Fan 7)—16 sts. Work Pat 2, place rem 2 sts on holder.

LEFT HAND
With A, pick up and k 1 st on top edge of Fan 8, using backward loop method cast on 6 sts (skip over rem edge sts of Fan 8), k 2 sts from Fan 6 holder, pick up and k 7 sts from edge of Fan 7—16 sts. Work Pat 2, place rem 2 sts on holder.
Fans 11-14 Work as for other fans, use Fan Diagram as guide.
Half fans 15 and 16
With A, pick up and k 16 sts along Fans 13 and 14 as for other Fans, work Pattern 3. Place rem 7 sts each on holders.

CUFFS
With RS facing, A and dpns, pick up and k 34 sts. Distribute evenly on 3 needles.
Rnd 1 (RS) Purl.
Rnd 2 Knit.
Rep rnds 1 and 2 twice. P 1 rnd. Bind off loosely.

With RS facing, A and dpn, beg at inside corner of palm, pick up and k 16 sts. Distribute evenly on 3 needles.

Rnds 1- 4 With B, knit.
Rnd 5 With A, knit.
Rnd 6 With A, purl.
Rep rnds 1-6 once more, then rnds 1 and 2.
Next rnd With B, [k2tog] 8 times—8 sts.
Next rnd With B, [k2tog] 4 times—4 sts.

Break yarn and fasten off rem 4 sts.

FELTING
Weave in loose ends. Turn mittens inside out and wash in hot water, cold rinse, with a drop or two of soap. Repeat washing until mittens shrink to desired size, it may take several wash cycles. Try them on periodically and when they fit your hands, turn them right side out and let them dry.

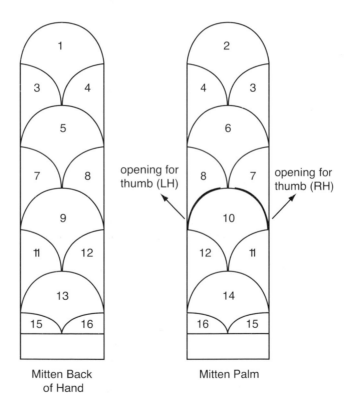

Mitten Back
of Hand

Mitten Palm

Toasty toes

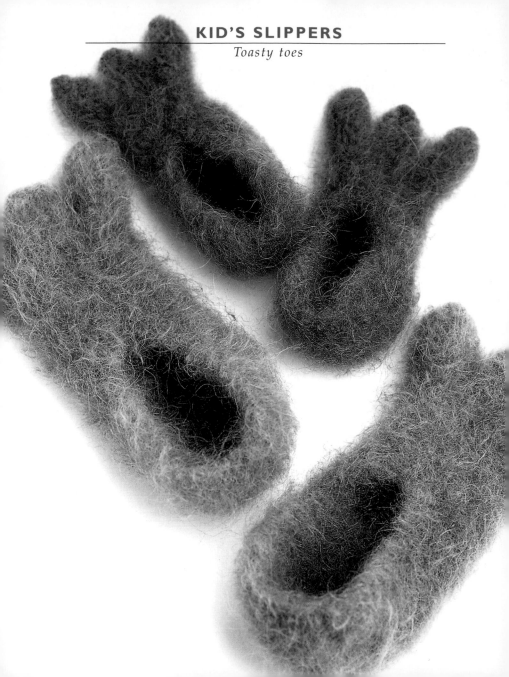

■■■■▶

What better way to warm up cold little toes than with these whimsical slippers? Designed by Susan Mills.

SIZES
■ To fit baby/toddler (kids)

Note
The amount of shrinkage during the felting process will determine the actual finished measurements.

MATERIALS
■ 1 3½oz/100g ball (each approx 110yd/100m) of JCA/Reynolds *Lopi* (wool) in #9983 apple green heather or #159 orchid
■ One pair size 13 (9mm) needles *or size to obtain gauge*
■ Stitch holders
■ Tapestry needle

GAUGE
10 sts and 13 rows = 4"/10cm over St st using size 13 (9mm) needles (before felting). *Take time to check gauge.*

HEEL
Cast on 32 (40) sts.

Row 1 (RS) K8 (10), pm, k16 (20), pm, k8 (10). P 1 row.

Next (dec) row (RS) [K to 3 sts before next marker, k2tog, k1, slip marker, k1, ssk] twice, k to end of row (4 sts dec'd). P 1 row.

Rep last 2 rows 1 (3) times more—24 sts.

Next (dec) row (WS) [P to 3 sts before next marker, p2tog tbl, p1, slip marker, p1, p2tog] twice, p to end.

Rep dec row every row until 8 sts rem. Bind off purlwise.

Piece, when stretched, should be a rectangle with the bound-off sts at the center of the bottom of rectangle with lines of decreasing slanting to the upper corners.

FOOT
Pick up and k 16 (21) sts along top of rectangle. Work in St st for 12 (20) rows, ending with a WS row.

TOES
K1 (2) and place on a holder.
*K next 5 (7) sts. Turn work.

For Baby/Toddler only
Next row (WS) P2, [M1, p1] 3 times— 8 sts.

For Kids only
Next row (WS) P1, [M1, p2] 3 times—10 sts.

For both sizes
Work in St st for 3 (7) rows, ending with a RS row.

Next row P2tog across—4 (5) sts.

For Baby/Toddler only
Next row (RS) K2tog twice—2 sts.

For Kids only
Next row (RS) K2tog, k1, k2tog—3 sts.

For both sizes
Cut yarn and fasten off*.
K 3 sts and place on a holder.

Rep between *'s over next 5 (7) sts. With other toes folded back and out of the way, pick up 1 (2) sts from first holder, 3 sts from center and last 1 (2) sts. Rep between *'s.

Sew center seam from top of middle toe until 1 (2)"/2.5 (5)cm from where first sts were cast-on to side of heel. Fold heel in half and sew bound-off sts tog. Sew center back heel seam.

FELTING

Place each slipper in a zippered pillowcase to eliminate shedding. Wash in a washing machine set to hot wash and cold rinse. Check every five to ten minutes until desired sized is achieved. It may be necessary to put items through this process two or three times depending on the water temperature and the amount of agitation. After felting, when still wet, try on slipper. Slipper can be stretched a bit if too much shrinkage has occurred. Repeat washing process if more shrinkage is desired. (Samples were washed twice.) Mold to desired shape/size and dry flat or tumble dry (additional shrinkage may occur if tumbled dry).

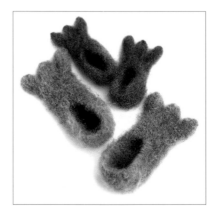

■■■▢

Reminiscent of swing coats from days past, this alpaca confection has a challenging structure with rewarding results. Designed by Bonnie Franz.

KNITTED MEASUREMENTS After felting
- Chest 22 (24, 26)"/56 (61, 66)cm
- Length 9 (10½, 13)"/23 (27, 33)cm
- Upper arm 8 (9, 11)"/20 (23, 28)cm

MATERIALS
- 4 1¾oz/50g balls (each approx 120yd/108m) of Blue Sky Alpacas *Alpaca DK* (alpaca) in #23 red
- One pair size 6 (4mm) needles *or size to obtain gauge*
- One size 6 (4mm) needle for 3-needle bind-off
- Stitch markers
- Two stitch holders
- Two ⅝"/15mm buttons
- Size G/6 (4mm) crochet hook

GAUGE
20 sts and 26 rows to 4"/10 cm over pat st using size 6 (4mm) needles (before felting). *Take time to check gauge.*

Note
Jacket is worked in one piece to armholes, then divided for back and fronts.

PATTERN STITCH
Row 1 (RS) Knit.
Row 2 *K1, p1; rep from * to end.
Rep rows 1 and 2 for pat st.

JACKET
Cast on 34 (37, 40) sts, pm, cast on 68 (74, 80) sts, pm, cast on 34 (37, 40) sts—136 (148, 160) sts. Work 46 (56, 68) rows in pat st, ending with a WS row.
Next row (RS) Work to first marker (left front), place rem sts on holder. Keeping to pat st, dec 1 st at neck edge every other row 8 (5, 6) times, then every 3rd row 4 (8, 10) times—22 (24, 24) sts. Work even until 80 (98, 116) rows from beg. Place sts on holder. Rejoin yarn to back 68 (74, 80) sts and work even in pat st until 80 (98, 116) rows from beg. Place these sts on holder. Rejoin yarn to right front and work as for left front, reversing neck shaping.

BIND OFF
With RS facing, place back 68 (74, 80) sts on one needle and 22 (24, 24) left front sts and 22 (24, 24) right front sts on 2nd needle, with both needles pointing in same direction. Work 3-needle bind-off over 1st 22 (24, 24) sts, regular bind-off for center back 24 (26, 32) sts and 3-needle bind-off for rem 22 (24, 24) sts.

SLEEVES
Cast on 40 (52, 64) sts. Work in pat st, inc 1 st each side every 6th (8th, 12th) row 6 times—52 (64, 76) sts. Cont in pat until 50 (56, 62) rows from beg. Bind off.

FINISHING
Sew top of sleeves to front and back armholes. Sew sleeve seams. With crochet hook, make two ch-8 button loop. Sew each

chain into a loop, place one just below front decrease and one approx 1¼ (2¼, 2¾)"/4.5 (5.5, 7)cm from cast-on edge.

FELTING

Fill sink with hot water and add baby jacket. Let soak for 30 minutes, or until saturated. Add more hot water and a small amount of soap. Agitate the jacket by rubbing and kneading, adding hot water as needed. When the fibers are matted and jacket is desired size, rinse in cool water to stop felting and remove soap. Roll in dry towel to remove excess water. Shape as desired and lay flat to dry.

Sew on buttons opposite loops.

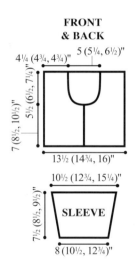

FRONT
& BACK

4¼ (4¾, 4¾)"   5 (5¼, 6½)"

5½ (6½, 7¼)"

7 (8½, 10½)"

13½ (14¾, 16)"

10½ (12¾, 15¼)"

SLEEVE

7½ (8½, 9½)"

8 (10½, 12¾)"

■■■▶

Gold and russet leaves, cut out of felted pieces of knitting, bring out the best of the season in this design by Bonnie Franz.

KNITTED MEASUREMENTS

- Before felting: 18"/45.5cm x 13¾"/35cm x 2"/5cm
- After felting approx 13"/33cm x 10"/25.5cm x 1"/2.5cm

MATERIALS

For Bag
- 2 4oz/113g skeins (each approx 190yd/173m) of Brown Sheep *Top of the Lamb Worsted* (wool) each in #240 fawn (MC) and #222 earth (A)
- One pair and one circular size 11 (8mm) circular needles 40"/100cm long *or size to obtain gauge*
- Tapestry needle
- Stitch marker

For leaves
- 1 1¾oz/50g skein (each approx 154yd/140m) of Brown Sheep *Top of the Lamb Sports Weight* (wool) each in #200 russet, #367 turkish olive and #416 harvest mustard for leaves
- One pair size 8 (5mm) needles *or size to obtain gauge*

GAUGE

For Bag
14 sts and 14 rnds to 4"/10cm over chart pat in Top of the Lamb using larger needles (before felting).

For Leaves
12 sts and 18 rnds to 4"/10cm over St st in Top of the Lamb Sports Weight using smaller needles before felting.
Take time to check gauge.

Note
Bag is knit in the round, then divided and worked back and forth in rows for the bottom. Always carry unused colors along back of work twisting every 3 or 4 sts.

BAG
With MC and circular needle, cast on 140 sts. Being careful not to twist sts, join to work in rounds, place marker at beg of rnd. Work in St st and chart pat, working 14-st rep 10 times. Rep rnds 1-16 three times, then rep rnds 1-8 once.

Shape bottom
Next rnd Bind off next 77 sts in pat and cont in chart rnd 9 over rem 63 sts.

Bottom flap
Working back and forth in rows, work chart rnds 10-16, then bind off in MC. With WS facing tog, sew bottom edges closed.

Straps (make 2)
With A and larger needles, cast on 8 sts. Work garter st for 100 rows. Bind off. Sew straps to top inside edge of bag, centering over second plaid and MC stripe.

LEAVES
Make 4 each russet and mustard, 6 of turkish olive. With smaller needles and Sports Weight, cast on 80 sts. Work 65 rows in St st. Bind off.

Put items in separate zippered pillowcases or mesh bags. Set washer for low water level and hottest temperature. Add small amount of soap and items to be felted. Put through wash cycle, checking felting progress often. When desired size, remove from machine and rinse in cool water to remove soap and to stop felting process.

Roll in dry towel to remove excess water. Shape as desired and gently stuff with a plastic bag to dry.

FINISHING

Cut one leaf from each rectangle, using template. Sew to top edge of bag using photo as a guide.

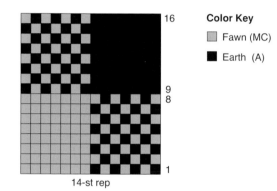

16

9
8

1

14-st rep

Color Key

☐ Fawn (MC)

■ Earth (A)

Actual Size

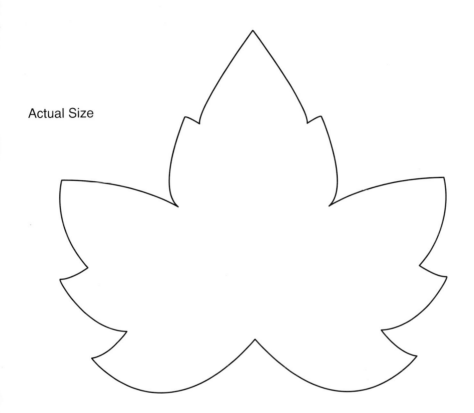

■ □ □ ▷

This funky scarf is hip fashion made easy. Just knit, felt, and cut. A Vogue Knitting original.

KNITTED MEASUREMENTS

■ After felting approx 60"/152cm long and 7"/18cm wide

MATERIALS

■ 3 1¾oz/50g skeins (each approx 83yd/76m) of Skacel Collections *Cashmere Tweed* (cashmere) in 600 dk green

■ One pair size 9 (5.5mm) needles *or size to obtain gauge*

GAUGE

18 sts = 4"/10cm over garter st using size 9 (5.5mm) needles (before felting).
Take time to check gauge.

Note

Scarf is knit in one piece, then felted. Fringe is cut from ends of felted fabric.

SCARF

Cast on 35 sts. Knit 320 rows. Bind off.

FELTING

Put scarf in zippered pillowcase or mesh bag. Set washer for low water level and hottest temperature. Add small amount of soap and scarf. Put through wash cycle, checking felting progress often. When desired size, remove from machine and rinse in cool water to remove soap and to stop felting process. Roll in dry towel to remove excess water. Shape and lay flat to dry.

FINISHING

When dry, cut ends of scarf into ten sections across bottom edges for fringe, each approx 6½"/16.5cm long and ¾"/2 cm wide.

FAIR ISLE HAT
Highland helmet

■■■■

With vibrant jewel tones, this time honored technique gets a modern make over. Designed by Sandi Prosser, its warmth and structure is ideal, whether you're making snowmen or taking to the slopes.

KNITTED MEASUREMENTS

■ Circumference before felting: approx 24¾"/63cm
■ Circumference after felting: approx 22"/55.5cm

MATERIALS

■ 1 1¾oz/50g ball (each approx 110yd/100m) of Naturally/SR Kertzer *Luxury DK* (wool/mohair) each in #990 teal (A), #993 evergreen (B), #992 spice (C), #914 sultan (D), #994 old gold (E), #1005 salmon (F), #1003 magenta (G), and #917 blossom (H)
■ One size 7 (4.5mm) circular needle, 16"/40cm long *or size to obtain gauge*
■ One set (4) dpn size 7 (4.5mm)
■ One pair size 7 (4.5mm) needles
■ Size G/6 (4mm) crochet hook
■ 10 stitch markers

GAUGE

19½ sts and 25 rows = 4"/10cm in St st over chart 1 using size 7 (4.5mm) circular needle (before felting).
Take time to check gauge.

Notes

1 Hat is worked in rnds on circular needle until too small to fit on circular needle, then worked on dpns. Knit every rnd of hat.
2 Ear flaps are worked back and forth in rows of garter st.

HAT

With A and circular needle, cast on 120 sts. Join, taking care not to twist sts on needle. Place marker for beg of rnd, and sl marker every rnd.
Rnds 1-3 With A, knit.
Rnds 4 and 5 *K2 A, k2 H; rep from * around.
Rnds 6 and 7 With A, knit.
Rnd 8 *K2 G, k2 A; rep from * around.
Rnd 9 With C, knit.
Rnd 10 With E, knit.
Rnds 11 and 12 With A, knit.
Rnd 13 With F, knit.
Beg chart 1
Rnds 14 - 27 Work chart 1, working 12-st rep 10 times.
Rnd 28 With E, knit.
Rnd 29 With G, knit.
Rnd 30 With B, knit.
Rnd 31 With C, knit.
Dec rnd 32 With C, k5, *k2tog, k10; rep from *, end last rep k5—110 sts.
Rnd 33 *K5 A, k5 F; rep from * around.
Dec rnd 34 With C, k 1 rnd, dec 2 sts evenly—108 sts.
Beg chart 2
Rnds 35-40 Work chart 2, working 6-st rep 18 times.
Dec rnd 41 *K1 A, k1 H; rep from *, AT SAME TIME, work decs as foll: k3, *ssk,

k2, k2tog, k6; rep from *, end last rep k3—
90 sts.

Rnd 42 With D, knit.

Dec rnd 43 With E, k2, *ssk, k2, k2tog, k4; rep from *, end k2—72 sts.

Rnd 44 With D, knit.

Dec rnd 45 With E, k1, *ssk, k2, k2tog, k2; rep from *, end k1—54 sts.

Dec rnd 46 With E, *ssk, k2, k2tog; rep from * around—36 sts.

Rnd 47 With A, knit.

Dec rnd 48 With A, *ssk, k2tog; rep from * around—18 sts.

Rnd 49 With A, knit.

Dec rnd 50 With A, *k2tog; rep from * around—9 sts.

Cut yarn leaving 6"/15.5cm tail and thread through rem 9 sts. Pull tight and secure end.

EAR FLAPS

With hat upside down, RS and center back facing, and A, beg in 19th st to the left of center back, pick up and k 21 sts.

Rows 1-5 With A, knit.

Rows 6-9 With B, knit.

Rows 10 and 11 With D, knit.

Rows 12 and 13 With E, knit.

Rows 14-17 With A, knit.

Dec row 18 With B, k2, ssk, k to last 4 sts, k2tog, k2—19 sts.

Row 19 With B, knit.

Rows 20-23 Rep row 18 and 19 twice—15 sts.

Rows 24 and 25 With G, rep rows 18 and 19—13 sts.

Rows 26-31 With A, rep rows 18 and 19 three times—7 sts.

Dec row 32 With A, k2, sl 1, k2tog, psso, k2—5 sts. Bind off.

Work 2nd ear flap to correspond to first one.

FINISHING

With RS facing and crochet hook, beg at center back lower edge of hat, work sc evenly around lower edge, alternating 1 st A, 1 st D.

FELTING

Set washer for hot wash, longest cycle and lowest water level. Add small amount of mild detergent. Do not use your washer's spin cycle. While agitating, check on the progress every 5 minutes. Set washer back to agitate longer if needed. When the hat is felted to the approx circumference, remove and rinse by hand in cool water. Roll in a towel to remove as much water as possible.

Chart 1

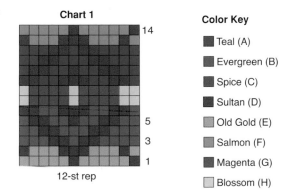

14

5

3

1

12-st rep

Color Key

- Teal (A)
- Evergreen (B)
- Spice (C)
- Sultan (D)
- Old Gold (E)
- Salmon (F)
- Magenta (G)
- Blossom (H)

Chart 2

6

1

6-st rep

BABY BLOCKS
Stackable fun

■■□▷

Build up your skills with Rebecca Rosen's striped blocks. A swift knit in stockinette stitch, these cuties are an easy, breezy treat for newbies.

KNITTED MEASUREMENTS
▪ Before felting: 5"/13cm x 5½"/14cm (each piece is rectangular before felting)
▪ After felting: 4"/10cm square

MATERIALS
▪ 1 3½oz /100g hank (each approx 127yd/114m) of Classic Elite Yarns *Montera* (llama/wool) in #3856 periwinkle, #3807 lavender, #3895 mauve, #3825 yellow, #3850 green, #3887 lime, #3829 dusty blue, #3831 turquoise
▪ One pair size 11 (8mm) needles *or size to obtain gauge*
▪ 1 large piece cardboard, measured to 4 x 4"/10 x 10cm squares for blocking
▪ Rustproof pins for blocking
▪ Fiberfill
▪ Tapestry needle

Notes
1 All blocks are knit in St st.
2 Each block is made of 6 squares: 3 solid, 1 two color/2-row stripe, 1 three color/4-row stripe, and 1 rainbow/2-row stripe. The squares are felted, then arranged randomly and stitched together in block shape.
3 Each square must be 4" x 4"/10 x 10cm after felting, so block carefully.

GAUGE
11 sts and 14 rows = 3¾"/9.5cm over St st (before felting).
Take time to check gauge.

COLOR PATTERNS
Solid square
Cast on 15 sts, work for 20 rows. Bind off loosely.
Two-color square
With first color, cast on 15 sts. Work 2 rows in each color until 20 rows have been worked. Bind off loosely.
Three-color square
With first color, cast on 15 sts. Follow color order, work 4 rows in each color until 20 rows have been worked. Bind off loosely.
Rainbow square
With first color cast on 15 sts. Follow color order, work 2 rows in each color until 20 rows have been worked. Bind off loosely.

BLOCK I
Solid square
Make 1 each: periwinkle, turquoise, dusty blue
Two color square
Dusty blue, mauve
Three color square
Sage, turquoise, yellow, turquoise, sage
Rainbow square
Lavender, sage, turquoise, dusty blue, yellow, lime, periwinkle, mauve, lavender, sage
Topstitching
Yellow

BLOCK 2
Solid square
Make 1 each: sage, lavender, mauve
Two-color square
Periwinkle, lime
Three-color square
Yellow, dusty blue, turquoise, dusty blue, yellow
Rainbow square
Lime, lavender, periwinkle, mauve, dusty blue, turquoise, yellow, sage, lime, lavender
Topstitching
Yellow

BLOCK 3
Solid square
Make 1 each: lime, yellow, lavender
Two-color square
Sage, dusty blue
Three-Color Square
Mauve, periwinkle, turquoise, periwinkle, mauve
Rainbow square
Periwinkle, lime, mauve, sage, lavender, yellow, dusty blue, turquoise, periwinkle, lime

Topstitching
Periwinkle

FELTING
Put squares in separate zippered pillowcases or mesh bags. Set washer for low water level and hottest temperature. Add small amount of soap and squares. Put through wash cycle, checking felting progress often. When desired size, remove from machine and rinse in cool water to remove soap and to stop felting process. Roll in dry towel to remove excess water. Pin each square to cardboard to exact 4"/10cm square measurement, let dry.

FINISHING
Assemble pieces into block shape. Using topstitch yarn as indicated, sew all but one seam closed. Fill block with fiberfill, sew rem seam closed. At each corner, sew all 3 sides tog, forming a triangular st. Rep for each block.

Baby pastels are a thing of the past with this bright blankie. A wonderful gift for any special delivery, it's also a great way for new knitters to become more comfortable with multiple colors. Designed by Gayle Bunn.

KNITTED MEASUREMENTS

- Before felting: 34½"/88cm x 36"/91.5cm
- After felting: approx 21"/53.5cm x 30"/76cm

MATERIALS

- 1 3½oz/100g skein (each approx 220yd/200m) of Cascade Yarns *Cascade 220* (wool) in #8010 cream (MC), #7805 pink (A), #7809 mauve (B), #7814 green (C), and #7825 orange (D)
- One size 8 (5mm) circular needle 36"/90cm long *or size to obtain gauge.*
- Tapestry needle

GAUGE

18 sts and 25 rows = 4"/10cm over St st using size 8 (5mm) needles (before felting). *Take time to check gauge*

Note

Blanket is worked lengthwise in rows of St st.

Stripe Pattern I

Rows I, 2 and 4 With A.
Rows 3 and 7 With C.
Rows 5 and 6 With B.
Row 8 With D.
Rep rows 1-8 for stripe pat 1.

Stripe Pattern 2

Row I With D.
Rows 2 and 5 With C.
Rows 3 and 4, 6 and 7 With MC.
Rows 8 and 9 With B.
Rows 10 and 11, 13 and 14 With MC.
Rows 12 and 15 With C.
Row 16 With D.
Rows 17 - 22 With A.
Rows 23 - 26 With MC.
Rows 27 - 28 With B.
Rep rows 1-28 for stripe pat 2.

BLANKET

With C, cast on 156 sts.
Next row (RS) With C, knit.
Next row With D, purl.
Cont in St st and rep stripe pat 1 five times, end with Row 6.
Cont in St st and rep stripe pat 2 three times.
Next row (RS) With D, knit.
Cont in St st and rep stripe pat 1 five times, end with Row 3.
With C, bind off.

Weave in ends. Set machine at lowest water level, hottest temp and highest agitation, add small amount of detergent and blanket. Begin washing, check on blanket frequently until felted. Remove blanket and rinse by hand in lukewarm water. Roll in towel to remove excess water. Dry flat.

FINISHING

When dry, work blanket st around edge with 2 strands A and tapestry needle.

SNOWFLAKE PILLOW

Nordic nights

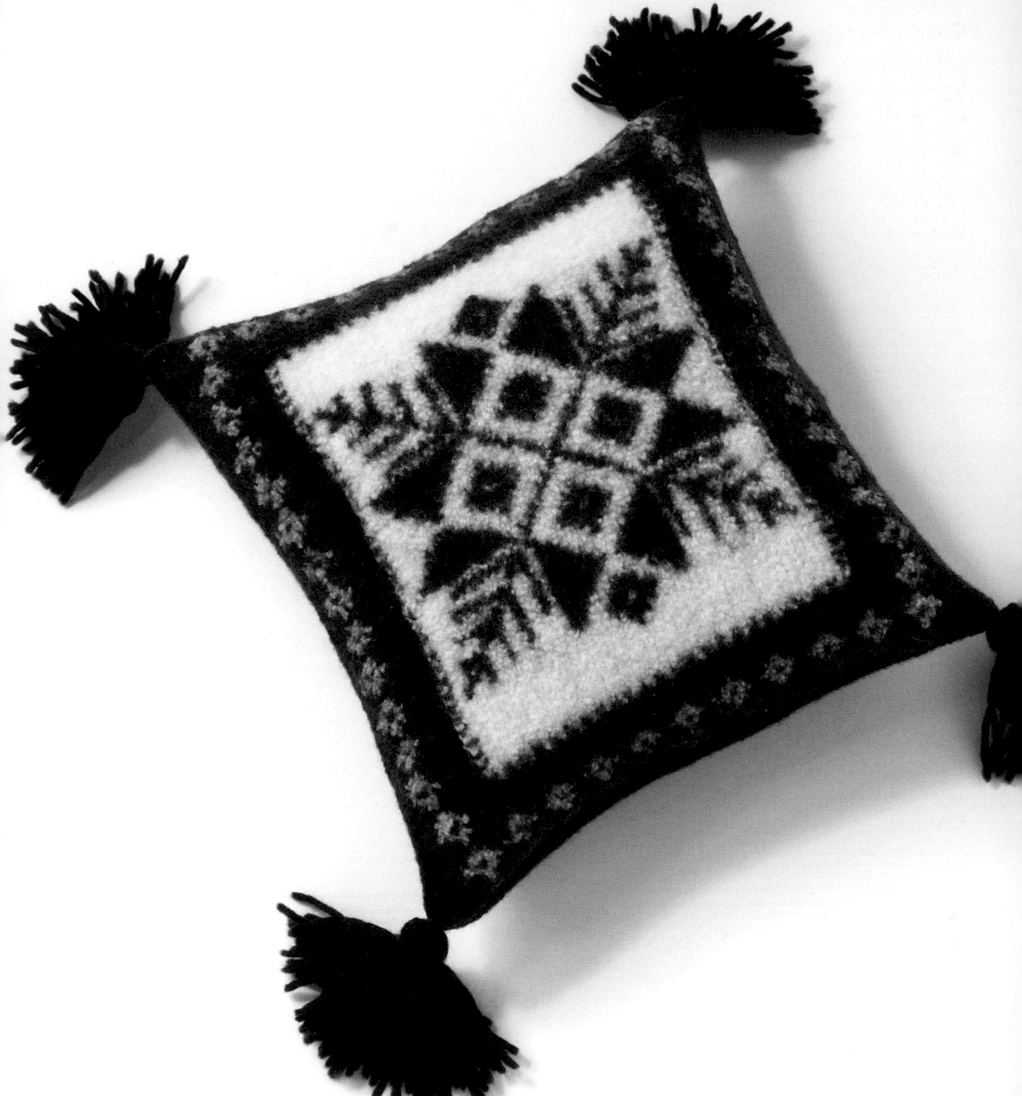

Gayle Bunn's tribute to Scandinavian design sparkles like snow under moonlight. A wonderful piece for the holidays, its cool, wintry center is warmed by golden borders.

KNITTED MEASUREMENTS

Before felting

■ Front 23½"/60cm x 23"/58cm

■ Back 24½"/62cm x 28"/71cm

After felting

■ Approx 16½"/42cm square

MATERIALS

■ 10 3½oz/100g balls (each approx 109yd/98m) of Crystal Palace Yarns *Iceland* (wool) in #3387 dark blue (MC)

■ 1 ball each in #1058 cream (A), #3433 brown (B) and #3549 and gold (C)

■ One pair size 10½ (6.5mm) needles *or size to obtain gauge*

■ One 16"/40cm square pillow form

■ Cardboard for tassel making 5"/12.5cm square

■ Tapestry needle

GAUGE

13 sts and 18 rows = 4"/10cm over St st using size 10½ (6.5mm) needles (before felting).

Take time to check gauge.

FRONT

With MC, cast on 77 sts. Work snowflake chart in St st for 103 rows. Bind off in MC.

BACK

With MC, cast on 80 sts. Work in St st for 130 rows. Bind off.

FELTING

Weave in ends. Set machine to lowest water level (just enough to cover pieces), hottest temperature, and highest agitation. Add pieces and small amount of liquid detergent. Begin washing and check on pillow pieces approx every 5 minutes until desired felting of fabric is achieved; the stitch definition should be almost unrecognizable. Remove pieces and rinse in lukewarm water. Roll pieces in towels to remove excess water. Dry flat.

TASSELS

(make 4)

Wind MC 35 times around cardboard. Cut yarn, leaving a 20"/51cm tail. With tapestry needle, wrap tail around all loops at top of cardboard and pull tightly. Slip yarn off cardboard and wrap tail around yarn several times approx ¾"/2cm below tied end. Draw needle through top of tassel, sew tassel to pillow corner.

FINISHING

When dry, front should measure approx 17"/43cm square, back should measure approx 18"/45.5cm by 21"/53.5cm. Cut back into 2 pieces, each approx 18"/45.5cm by 10½"/26.5cm. Mark 3 buttonholes across long edge of one back piece 1"/2.5cm in from edge as foll: 1 buttonhole in center, rem 2 buttonholes 5"/12.5cm on either side of center. Cut each buttonhole slightly shorter than the button. With MC and tapestry needle, work blanket st around each hole. Sew buttons opposite holes on other piece of back. Close buttons. Pin tog over-lapping edges between buttonholes. With right sides facing, and buttons in center, pin front and back tog. Trim excess from back. Sew front and back tog. Trim overlap to match front, remove pins. Sew tassels to each corner. Insert pillow form.

Color Key

■ Dark Blue (MC)

☐ Cream (A)

■ Brown (B)

▨ Gold (C)

103
100

90

80

70

60

50

40

30

20

10

1

Start Here

ADULT'S SLIPPERS

Fuzzy feet

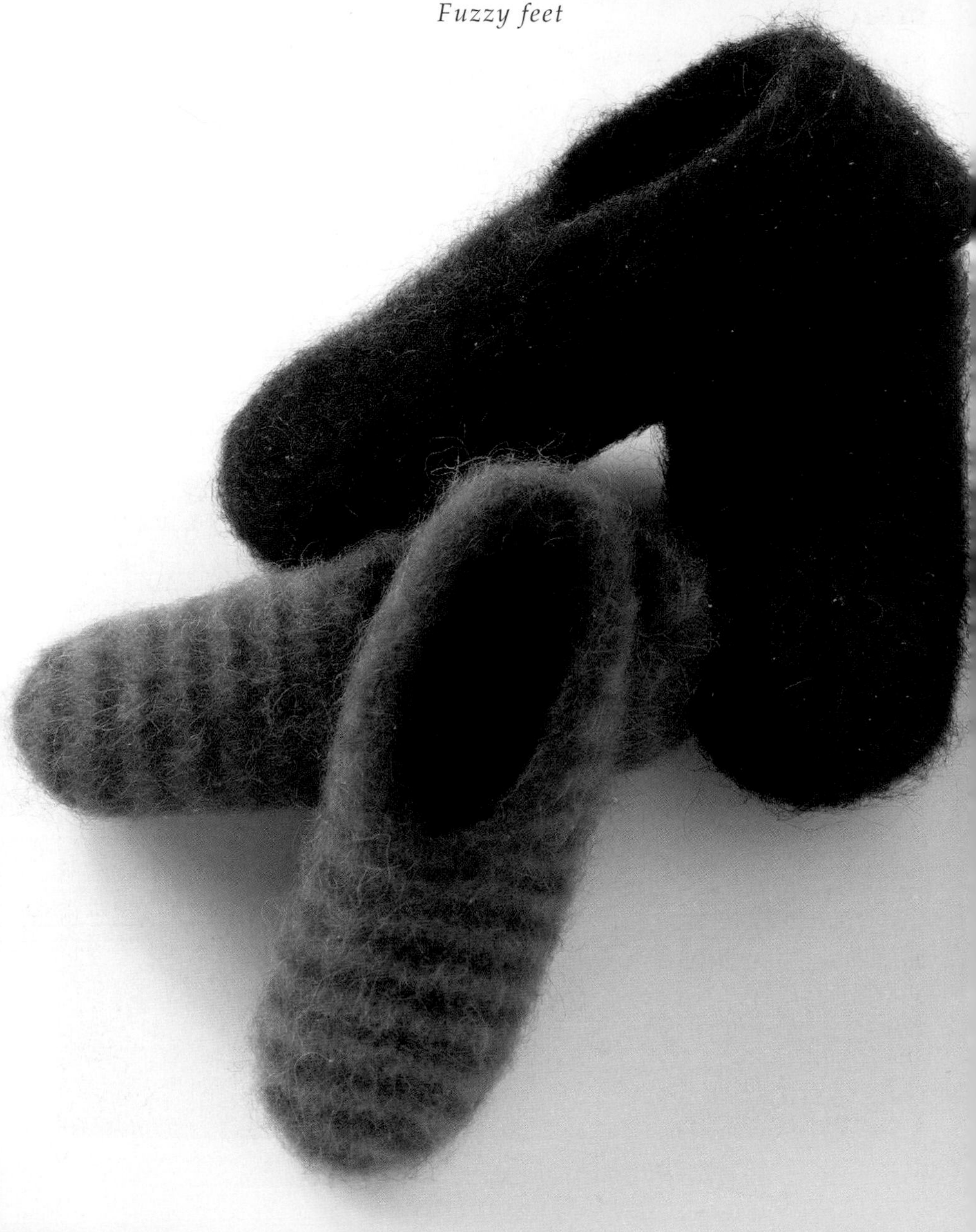

■■■■▶

Straightforward stockinette stitch stripes and a few strategic decreases make slipping your tired feet into something more comfortable. Designed by Mags Kandis.

SIZES

Woman's version
■ To fit women's sizes 5/6 (7/8, 9/10)
Man's version
■ To fit men's sizes 7/8 (9/10, 11/12)

MATERIALS

Woman's version
■ 1 3½oz/100g skeins (each approx 110 yd/100m) of Reynolds *Lopi* (wool) in #307 lt pink (A) and #910 dk pink (B)
Man's version
2 skeins in #911 brown
Both versions
■ One pair size 10½ (7mm) needles or *size to obtain gauge*
■ One set (4) size 10½ (7mm) dpn

GAUGE

12 sts and 17 rows = 4"/10cm over St st using size 10½ (7mm) needles (before felting).
Take time to check gauge.

Stripe Pat woman's slipper only
Row 1 (RS) With B, knit.
Row 2 With B, purl
Row 3 With A, knit.
Row 4 With A, purl.
Rep rows 1-4 for stripe pat.

WOMAN'S SLIPPERS

With straight needles and A, cast on 28 sts.
Next row (RS) Knit.
Next row Purl.
Work in stripe pat until 30 rows have been completed, cast on 4 sts at end of last row— 32 sts.
Next row (RS) With RS facing, divide sts evenly and place on 3 dpn. Being careful not to twist sts, join and pm to mark beg rnd. Cont in stripe pat and knit every rnd until 20 (24, 29) rnds have been completed.
Shape toe
Next rnd [K6, k2tog] 4 times— 28 sts.
Next rnd [K5, k2tog] 4 times—24 sts.
Cont to dec 4 sts in this way, working 1 less st before each k2tog on every rnd until 8 sts rem.
Next rnd K2tog 4 times—4 sts. Cut tail 11"/28cm long, thread through rem 4 sts and secure. With RS facing tog, fold cast-on edge of slipper in half and sew closed to form back heel. Weave in ends.
Edging
With RS facing, dpn and B, pick up and knit 44 sts around foot opening. K 1 rnd, p 1 rnd. Bind off knitwise.

MAN'S SLIPPERS

With straight needles, cast on 32 sts. Work in St st until 34 rows have been completed, cast on 8 sts at end of last row—40 sts
Next row (RS) With RS facing, divide sts evenly and place on 3 dpn. Being careful not to twist sts, join and pm to mark beg rnd. Knit until 28 (32, 36) rnds have been completed.

Shape toe

Next rnd [K8, k2tog] 4 times—36 sts.

Next rnd [K7, k2tog] 4 times—32 sts.
Cont to dec 4 sts in this way, working 1 less st before each k2tog on every round until 8 sts rem.

Next rnd K2tog 4 times—4 sts. Cut tail 11"/28cm long, thread through rem 4 sts and secure. With RS facing tog, fold cast-on edge of slipper in half and sew closed to form back heel. Weave in ends.

Edging

Work as for women's version, using A and picking up 50 sts.

Put items in separate zippered pillowcases or mesh bags. Set washer for medium water level and hottest temperature. Add small amount of soap, a towel or pair of jeans for agitation, and items to be felted. Put through wash cycle, checking felting progress often. When desired size, remove felted item from machine and rinse in cool water to remove soap and to stop felting process. Roll in dry towel to remove excess water. Shape as desired and gently stuff with a plastic bag to dry.

Washington Square

■■□□

At home, in the city or the country, this clever faux-patchwork purse captures the vibrant colors of Autumn. Designed by Mags Kandis.

KNITTED MEASUREMENTS

▪ Before felting: 13½"/34cm x 19"/48cm

▪ After felting: approx 10"/25.5cm x 11"/28cm

MATERIALS

▪ 1 3½oz/100g balls (each approx 223yd/204m) of Patons *Classic Wool* (wool) each in #204 gold (A), #231 chestnut brown (B), #206 russet (C), #238 paprika (D) and #221 forest green (E)

▪ One pair size 10½ (6.5mm) needles *or size to obtain gauge*

▪ Tapestry needle

GAUGE

15 sts and 21 rows to 4"/10cm over St st using size 10½ (6.5mm) needles (before felting). *Take time to check gauge*

Side 1

With A, cast on 50 sts loosely. Work in St st for 50 rows. Change to B and cont in St st for 50 more rows. Bind off loosely.

Side 2

With C, cast on 50 sts loosely. Work in St st for 50 rows. Change to D and cont in St st for 50 more rows. Bind off loosely.

STRAPS (make 2)

With E, cast on 5 sts loosely. Work in St st for 50"/172cm. Bind off.

FINISHING

With RS facing tog, sew side 1 and side 2 tog along side edges using mattress st and matching color changes. With RS facing tog, fold bag so that joined seams are at center of front and back of bag. Sew bottom edge closed. Weave in all ends.

FELTING

Put bag and straps in separate zippered pillowcases or mesh bags. Set washer for medium water level and hottest tempera-

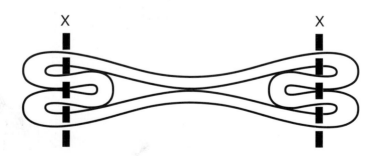

ture. Add small amount of soap, a towel or pair of jeans for agitation, and items to be felted. Put through wash cycle, checking felting progress often. When desired size, remove felted item from machine and rinse in cool water to remove soap and to stop felting process. Roll in dry towel to remove excess water. Shape as desired and gently stuff with a plastic bag to dry.

STRAP HOLES

Insert knitting needle through all four layers of fold as shown in the diagram. Wiggle the needle around to open up and stretch the holes. With front side of bag facing, insert end of one strap into hole, pull through to middle of fold. Insert one end of other strap into same hole from back side of bag to middle of fold. Knot ends tog in middle of fold. Repeat on other side of bag.

■■■▶

Liven up afternoon tea with this kaleido-scopic kettle cover by Susan Guagliumi. Ribbons and buttons inspire "Alice in Wonderland" whimsy, while short row wrapping creates a snug-yet-comfortable fit.

KNITTED MEASUREMENTS
▪ Finished measurements to fit 10-cup pot
▪ After felting: Approx 10"/25.5cm high and 22"/56cm circumference, lower edge can be cuffed for shorter pot.

MATERIALS
▪ 2 1¾oz/50 g skeins (each approx 109yd/100m) of Noro/Knitting Fever, Inc., *Kureyon* (wool) in #126
▪ One pair size 11 (8mm) needles *or size to obtain gauge*
▪ 4 yd/4m scrap yarn
▪ 40-50 buttons, assorted sizes and colors
▪ 2yd/2m ⅛"–¼"/3mm–6mm ribbon
▪ Yarn needle
▪ Sewing needle and thread
▪ Crochet hook size F/5 (3.75mm)

GAUGE
14 sts = 4"/10cm over St st using size 11 (8mm) needles (before felting).
Take time to check gauge.

Note
The tea cozy is knit in short rows. Be sure to knit the wrapped st tog with the wrap when increasing the number of worked sts. The slits for handle and spout are posi-tioned at about the middle of the cozy. For very high spouts, adjust accordingly when seaming cozy.

SHORT ROW WRAPPING
(wrap and turn - w&t)
Knit side
1 Wyib, sl next st purlwise.
2 Move yarn between the needles to the front.
3 Sl the same st back to LH needle. Turn work, bring yarn to the p side between nee-dles. One st is wrapped. When short rows are completed, work to just before wrapped st, insert RH needle under the wrap and knitwise into the wrapped st, k them tog.
Purl side
1 Wyif, sl next st purlwise.
2 Move yarn between the needles to the back of work.
3 Sl same st back to LH needle. Turn work, bring yarn back to the p side between the needles. One st is wrapped. When short rows are completed, work to just before wrapped st, insert RH needle from behind into the back lp of the wrap and place on LH needle; P wrap tog with st on needle.

TEA COZY
With scrap yarn, cast on 49 sts and k 2 rows. Cut scrap yarn.
With MC, p 1 row.
Beg short row decrease
*Row 1 (RS) Knit 46 sts, w &t.
Row 2 and all WS rows (unless otherwise specified) Purl to end of needle.

Row 3 K43, w & t.
Row 5 K40, w & t.
Row 7 K37, w & t.
Row 9 K34, w & t.
Row 11 K31, w & t.
Shape cozy
Row 13 K28, w & t.
Row 14 P18, w & t.
Row 15 K15, w & t.
Row 16 P5, w & t.
Beg short row incs.
Row 17 K9, w & t.
Row 18 P20, w & t.
Row 19 K24, w & t.
Row 20 P33 (to end of needle).
Row 21 K36, w & t.
Row 22 and all WS rows Purl to end of needle.
Row 23 K39, w & t.
Cont working 3 more sts each knit row until 48 sts are active. Wrap, but do not knit the 49th st, purl to end.*
Rep from * to * twice more.

Handle opening
Next row (RS) K18, bind off 18 sts, k13 sts.

Next row P13, cast on 18 sts, p18.
Rep from * to * three times more.
Knit 2 rows with scrap yarn. Bind off.

FINISHING
Lightly press scrap rows so they lay flat. Fold back scrap knitting. Thread sewing needle with MC. Beg at widest edge (bottom of cozy), graft seam for 18 sts. Cut yarn and beg at top of cozy, graft seam for 13 sts. With crochet hook, work 1 row sc to bind off rem sts for spout. Clip and remove scrap knitting. Work in all ends.

FELTING
Soak cozy in hot water for 10 minutes. Wash in machine with 2 pairs of jeans, hottest water and detergent. If necessary, shrink further by finishing in the dryer. Sew on buttons and thread ribbon through buttons and tie bows, then knot bows to make secure.

DECORATING
Sew on buttons and thread ribbon through buttons, then tie ribbons in bows. Make knots in bows to secure.

DOG COAT
Puppy love

■■■▢

Protect your best friend from the elements with this dog-friendly jacket by Gayle Bunn. Overhand stitching detail makes for maximum cuteness while velcro closure ensures minimum effort.

KNITTED MEASUREMENTS

■ To fit a small dog. Measuring from dog's neck to beginning of tail approximately 12"/30.5 cm

MATERIALS

■ 3 3½ oz/100g balls (each approx 210yd/190m) of Plymouth *Galway* (wool) in #13 purple (MC)

■ 1 ball each in #16 red (A), #9 black (B) and #1 cream (C)-for embroidery

■ One pair size 8 (5mm) needles *or size to obtain gauge*

■ 3 sets ¾"/2cm "coin set" round Velcro fasteners

■ Embroidery needle

GAUGE

18 sts and 25 rows to 4"/10cm over St st using size 8 (5 mm) needles (before felting). *Take time to check gauge.*

Note

When finished you will have two pieces of felted fabric. One piece of MC will be cut into shapes for coat body and straps. One piece of A will be cut into heart shape.

BODY AND STRAPS

With MC, cast on 111 sts. Work in St st until piece measures 28"/71cm from beg, end with a WS row. Bind off.

HEART

With A, cast on 24 sts. Work in St st until piece measures 5"/12.5cm from beg, end with a WS row. Bind off.

FINISHING

Weave in all ends.

FELTING

Set your washing machine at lowest water level (just enough to cover pieces), hottest temperature and highest agitation. Add pieces and a small amount of liquid detergent. Begin washing and check on pieces approx every 5 minutes until desired felting is achieved; the stitch definition should be almost unrecognizable. Remove pieces and rinse by hand in lukewarm water. Roll pieces in towels to remove excess water. Dry flat.

CUTTING SHAPES

Using template provided on next page, enlarge to full size and trace body and straps shapes onto felted pieces of MC, cut out. Trace heart shape onto felted piece of A, cut out. With B, embroider blanket stitch around heart and outer edges of body and straps. Sew heart onto body as shown. Trace "love" onto body as shown. With C, stitch over "love" using outline stitch. Position straps in middle of coat body, sew into place. Sew one set of Velcro fasteners onto straps. Sew 2 sets of Velcro fasteners onto neck extension.

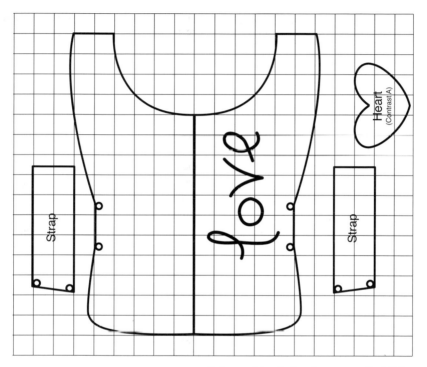

Enlarge grid so that each square = 1inch/2.5cm

RESOURCES

US RESOURCES

Write to the yarn companies listed below for purchasing and mail-order information.

BERROCO, INC.
14 Elmdale Road
P.O. Box 367
Uxbridge, MA 01569

BLUE SKY ALPACA
P.O. Box 387
St Francis, MN 55070

BROWN SHEEP CO.
100662 County Road 16
Mitchell, NE 69357

CASCADE YARNS, INC.
1224 Andover Park E
Tukwila, WA 98188-3905

CLASSIC ELITE YARNS
300 Jackson Ave.
Lowell, MA 01854

CRYSTAL PALACE YARNS
2320 Bissell Ave.
Richmond, CA 94804

COLINETTE
Distributed by
Unique Kolours

DALE OF NORWAY, INC.
N16 W23390 Stoneridge Drive
Suite A
Waukesha, WI 53188

JCA
35 Scales Lane
Townsend, MA 01469

KNITTING FEVER, INC.
P.O. Box 502
Roosevelt, NY 11575

LA LANA WOOLS
136 Paseo Norte
Taos, NM 87571

MUENCH YARNS
1323 Scott Street
Petaluma, CA 94954

MANOS DEL URUGUAY
P.O. Box 770
Medford, MA 02155

NATURALLY
distributed by
S.R. Kertzer, Ltd.

NORO
Distributed by
Knitting Fever, Inc.

PATONS®
P.O. Box 40
Listowel, ON N4W 3H3
Canada

PLYMOUTH YARNS
P.O. Box 28
Bristol, PA 19007

REYNOLDS
Distributed by JCA

ROWAN YARNS
4 Townsend West, Unit 8
Nashua, NH 03063

SKACEL COLLECTION
P.O. Box 88110
Seattle, WA 98138-2110
(800) 255-1278

S. R. KERTZER, LTD.
50 Trowers Road
Woodbridge, ON L4L 7K6
Canada

TAHKI·STACY CHARLES, INC.
70-30 80th Street
Building #36
Ridgewood, NY 11385

TAHKI YARNS
Distributed by
Tahki·Stacy Charles, Inc.

CANADIAN RESOURCES

Write to US resources for mail-order availability of yarns not listed.

BERROCO, INC.
distributed by
S. R. Kertzer, Ltd.

DIAMOND YARN
9697 St. Laurent
Montreal, PQ H3L 2N1
and
155 Martin Ross, Unit #3
Toronto, ON M3J 2L9

LES FILS MUENCH, CANADA
5640 rue Valcourt
Brossard, PQ J4W 1C5

MUENCH YARNS, INC.
distributed by
Les Fils Muench, Canada

NATURALLY
distributed by
S. R. Kertzer, Ltd.

PATONS ®
PO Box 40
Listowel, ON N4W 3H3

ROWAN
distributed by
Diamond Yarn

S. R. KERTZER, LTD.
105A Winges Rd.
Woodbridge, ON L4L 6C2

UK RESOURCES

Not all yarns used in this book are available in the UK. For yarns not available, make a comparable substitute or contact the US manufacturer for purchasing and mail-order information.

ROWAN YARNS
Green Lane Mill
Holmfirth
West Yorks HD7 1RW
Tel: 01484-681881

SILKSTONE
12 Market Place
Cockermouth
Cumbria, CA13 9NQ
Tel: 01900-821052

THOMAS RAMSDEN GROUP
Netherfield Road
Guiseley
West Yorks LS20 9PD
Tel: 01943-872264

VOGUE KNITTING FELTING

Editorial Director
TRISHA MALCOLM

Yarn Editor
VERONICA MANNO

Art Director
CHI LING MOY

Production Manager
DAVID JOINNIDES

Executive Editor
CARLA S. SCOTT

Photography
QUENET STUDIOS

Book Managers
SHANNON KERNER
MICHELLE LO

Photo Stylist
LAURA MAFFEO

Graphic Designer
CAROLINE WONG

President, Sixth&Spring Books
ART JOINNIDES

Instructions Editors
LISA PAUL
VICTORIA HILDITCH

LOOK FOR THESE OTHER TITLES IN
THE *VOGUE KNITTING ON THE GO!* SERIES...